7 FORGOTTEN WONDERS of the WORLD

Vikas khatri

Published by:

F-2/16, Ansari Road, Daryaganj, New Delhi-110002
☎ 011-23240026, 011-23240027 • *Fax:* 011-23240028
Email: info@vspublishers.com • *Website:* www.vspublishers.com

Regional Office : Hyderabad
5-1-707/1, Brij Bhawan (Beside Central Bank of India Lane)
Bank Street, Koti, Hyderabad - 500 095
☎ 040-24737290
E-mail: vspublishershyd@gmail.com

Branch Office : Mumbai
Jaywant Industrial Estate, 2nd Floor–222, Tardeo Road
Opposite Sobo Central Mall, Mumbai – 400 034
☎ 022-23510736
E-mail: vspublishersmum@gmail.com

Follow us on:

All books available at **www.vspublishers.com**

© Copyright: V&S PUBLISHERS
Edition - 2017

The Copyright of this book, as well as all matter contained herein (including illustrations) rests with the Publishers. No person shall copy the name of the book, its title design, matter and illustrations in any form and in any language, totally or partially or in any distorted form. Anybody doing so shall face legal action and will be responsible for damages.

Prologue

Earth is a very beautiful planet. It has a store of treasures that can never be exhausted. The treasures of Earth are precious like gold and diamonds, but more precious than these are the treasures that fill a man with amazement, wonder, surprise and joy. The wonders of the Earth are many and of many kinds. Some of them are natural – nature formed them over time in a way that is beyond understanding.

Geothermal phenomena, like deep sea vents, volcanoes and waterfalls are of breathtaking beauty. Images of oneself haloed by rainbows formed high in the sky, take one's breath away. One can look and wonder at the marvels of the nature.

Some of the wonders are architectural marvels which, account for the brilliance of the human mind, its perceptive power and adroit endeavors. These were considered as some of the **greatest wonders of the world**, but not great enough to leave behind an indelible impression on human mind, they were lost to the other greater and stupendous works of the human imagination. The **momentous works** of art as and architecture by the humans and their ability to capture in realistic frame have baffled travellers and onlookers from times immemorial. With the advance of the science and technology, engineering skills and **construction facilities**, the human hands, out of there minds began to carve, edifices which made the world more pleasant and beautiful.

This book aims to present before the reader, 'a few' of the countless wonders our planet has to offer us.

Seven Forgotten Underwater Wonders of the World

A noted marine explorer named Jacques-Yves Cousteau wrote: *"It is all strange, unearthly, and yet familiar. Strange because the sea, once it casts its spell, holds one in its net of wonders forever."*

Diving is becoming a much more popular sport as humans become more fascinated with the diverse ecosystems of the deep. Coral reefs, like many of these underwater wonders, are structures built by living organisms. Second only to tropical rain forests in biodiversity, coral reefs provide homes for thousands of species. Unfortunately, they are at risk all around the world.

To promote awareness of the fragile marine ecosystem, CEDAM International - an organization dedicated to conservation, education, diving, and marine research - began the Seven Wonders of the World project in 1989. The message was simple: If underwater wonders are not protected, they will be lost forever. After considering sites around the world, CEDAM chose Palau, the Belize Barrier Reef, the Galapagos Islands, the Northern Red Sea, Lake Baikal, the Great Barrier Reef, and the Deep Sea Vents. Each was selected on the basis of its natural beauty, unique marine life, scientific research value, environmental significance, and whether it is representative of an overall area.

By focusing on these seven sites, CEDAM hopes to promote the protection of all underwater wonders. *"We are the first generation to explore the wonders of the underwater world,"* says George Page, host of the public television series Nature. *"Let's hope we are not the last."*

Palau

Palau (Palauan *Belau*), republic, W Pacific Ocean, comprises more than 300 islands, islets, and atolls of the Caroline group. Major islands include Koror, the current seat of government, and Babelthuap, the future capital. Area of the republic, 487 sq km (188 sq mi). Of the total population (1990, 15,122), ethnic Palauans make up about 83%; minority groups include Filipinos and Chinese. Palauan and English are the official languages. Leading occupations include fishing and subsistence agriculture; the country relies heavily on aid from the U.S. The U.S. dollar is the legal currency. Palau has a presidential system with a bicameral legislature.

Palau

Spain formally claimed the Palau Islands in 1885 but sold them to Germany 14 years later. Japan seized them in 1914 and established a naval base. The islands were captured by American forces in 1944, during World War II. After the war they became part of the Trust Territory of the Pacific Islands, administered by the U.S. under UN supervision. In 1980 the islands adopted a republican constitution. During the next ten years, a compact of free association granting Palau independence, but with defense remaining the responsibility of the U.S., was repeatedly submitted to referendum. The measure was supported by a majority of Palauan voters, but not by the 75 percent required to overcome a constitutional ban on port calls by U.S. nuclear-armed vessels. After a constitutional amendment eased this requirement, the compact passed in 1993. Palau became independent on Oct. 1, 1994, and was admitted to the UN in December.

The Belize Barrier Reef

The second largest barrier reef in the world rises from the seafloor off the coast of Belize. A diver's paradise, it is known for fascinating coral formations, myriad fish and invertebrates, and exceptional water clarity.

The Belize Barrier Reef

On the ocean side of this 160-mile-long reef is a popular tourist designation known as Lighthouse Reef. Here, crystal-clear waters fill the famous Blue Hole, a crater more than 1,000 feet across and just over 400 feet deep. At the surface, healthy coral formations rim this wonder within a wonder, but at a depth of 125 feet, neither corals nor fish can be found. Instead, a diver finds stalactites formed during the Ice Age, when the world sea level was much lower and the Blue Hole was a subterranean cavern. The hole formed when the cavern's roof collapsed.

To the south is Glover's Reef, surrounded by waters so clear that visibility even at night is quite good: The long shaft of a diver's torch can pierce the water to a distance of 15 feet. Because it is several miles from the mainland, this reef is not affected by silt and sediment runoff. At Glover's, the arrival of a diver startles bright red cardinalfish swimming in open water, they rely on organs called lateral lines running along both sides of their bodies. A combination of sonar and radar, a lateral line senses vibrations and movements in the water, allowing fish to detect predators and pray. It's also an early warning device. As a fish swims, it creates a sort of bow wake that bounces off solid objects. When another fish feels the wake, it moves to avoid a collision.

Glover's Reef is home to the Emerald Forest, a site named for magnificent elk horn coral "trees" having trunks a foot diametre and canopies more than ten feet high. Several kinds of exotic fish also live here, and at night, a camera-bearing diver can catch them asleep, tucked in against the reef, but still out in the open. Butterflyfish as colourful as backyard butterflies hover in the water. So do hogfish with pig like snouts, trumpetfish that look like two-foot-long musical instruments, and parrotfish, their beaklike mouths closed for the night.

Not all of the reef's creatures are lost in sleep, however. Manta rays and sharks prowl the darkness, seeking meals. Lobsters, crabs, shrimp, and nudibranchs (the beautiful slugs of the sea) search the reef for food and mates. A Nassau grouper gets its mouth "cleaned" by a tiny shrimp, which darts from side to side and from top to bottom to remove small parasites and dead flesh from the cooperative fish, its mouth frozen in a wide yawn. The shrimp gets a free meal, so to speak. Dr. Mary Wicksten, a marine biologist at Texas A&M University and a specialist in these so-called cleaning stations, says that fish seek out established stations on the reef because the activity is important for their health. Like several other reef fish, the Nassau grouper is remarkable for its ability to change sex as it gets older, increasing its chances for reproductive success when another grouper is met.

At a natural cut in Glover's Reef, where water surges during the changing of the tide, a diver can free-fall horizontally, whipped along by the strong current. But fish hover without obvious effort, their streamlined bodies designed by nature to keep them in place in such conditions. Jutting from the walls of the cut, like fingers on a huge hand, are lavender tube sponges that eat by filtering tiny plants and animals from the sea. Soft coral sea fans, also filter feeders, bend in the breeze like underwater current that brings them a constant supply of food. The dominant life-form here is the hard coral, which is capable of withstanding the force of very strong wave action.

Where the current exits this canyon, it stirs up sand from the floor of a lagoon, reducing visibility. Somewhere near the bottom, turtles and manatees leisurely feed on sea grasses, while small coral heads form mini-reefs alive with tiny fish.

Across the lagoon is the Hol Chan Marine Reserve, a small area off Ambergris Cay where the tangled roots of a mangrove forest reach into the water. Even here, small fish dart among the roots, looking for meals or protection from predators.

Hol Chan, which is Maya for "the cut," was established in 1987. It encompasses all three habitats of the barrier reef ecosystem: reef, lagoon, and mangroves. Although separate, each area depends on the others. Marine scientist Jacque Carter, who has long studied Belize's fish, writes: "The mangroves are a feeding and breeding ground for reef fishes; they also trap silt and sediment runoff before it reaches the reef. The lagoon is...a feeding ground for many reef fishes, and the sea grasses... trap reef-smothering particles [keeping them] from reaching the lagoon, mangroves and shore areas from destructive wave action. If one area is damaged, the others are also affected – which is why it is important to protect the entire system, and not just the beautiful coral reef."

The Galapagos Islands

Galápagos Islands or Colón Archipelago, group of islands, Ecuador, in the Pacific Ocean, constituting a province of the country, about 965 km (about 600 mi) off the W coast. The archipelago consists of six larger and numerous smaller islands lying on or near the equator. The principal islands are Isabela, San Cristóbal, Fernandina, San Salvador, Santa María, and Santa Cruz. The total land area is 8010 sq km (3093 sq mi).

The Galapagos Islands

The islands are volcanic in origin, with level shorelines and mountainous interiors culminating in high central craters, some of which rise more than 1520 m (5000 ft) above sea level. Several volcanoes are active. The islands are fringed with mangroves; farther inland, although still in coastal regions, where little rain falls, the vegetation consists chiefly of thorn trees, cactus, and mesquite. In the uplands, which are exposed to a heavy mist, the flora is more luxuriant. The climate and the temperature of the waters surrounding the islands are modified by the cold Humboldt Current from the Antarctic.

The Galápagos group is noted for its fauna, which includes numerous animals found only in the archipelago and different subspecies on separate islands. Unique to the archipelago are six species of giant tortoise (Span. *galápago*—thus the islands' name). Other reptiles on the islands include two species of large lizards of the iguana family: a burrowing land lizard and an unusual marine lizard that dives into the ocean for seaweed. The islands contain as many as 85 different species of birds, including flamingos, flightless cormorants, finches, and penguins. Sea lions are numerous, as are many different shore fish. Part of the Galápagos is a wildlife sanctuary.

The Northern Red Sea

The Red Sea is a salt water inlet of the Indian Ocean between Africa and Asia. The connection to the ocean is in the south through the Bab el Mandeb sound and the Gulf of Aden. In the north are the Sinai Peninsula, the Gulf of Aqaba, and the Gulf of Suez.

The Northern Red Sea

Occupying a part of the Great Rift Valley, the Red Sea has a surface area of about 438,000 km² (169,100 square miles). It is roughly 2250 km (1398 mi) long and, at its widest point at 355 km (220.6 miles) wide. It has a maximum depth of 2211 m (7254 ft) in the central median trench and an average depth of 490 m (1,608 feet), but there are also extensive shallow shelves, noted for their marine life and corals. The sea is the habitat of over 1,000 invertebrate species and 200 soft and hard corals and is the world's northernmost tropical sea.

The Red Sea lies between arid land, desert and semi-desert. The main reasons for the better development of reef systems along the Red Sea is because of its greater depths and an efficient water circulation pattern, The Red Sea water mass exchanges its water with the Arabian Sea, Indian Ocean via the Gulf of Aden. The Red Sea is one of the most saline water bodies in the world, due to the effects of the water circulation pattern, resulting from evaporation and wind stress. Salinity ranges between 3.6 and 3.8%.

The climate of the Red Sea is the result of two distinct monsoon seasons; a northeasterly monsoon and a southwesterly monsoon. Monsoon winds occur because of the differential heating between the land surface and sea. Very high surface temperatures coupled with high salinities makes this one of the hottest and saltiest bodies of seawater in the world. The average surface water temperature of the Red Sea during the summer is about 26 °C (79 °F) in the north and 30 °C (86 °F) in the south, with only about 2 °C (3.6 °F) variation during the winter months. The overall average water temperature is 22 °C (72 °F). The scarcity of rainfall and no major source of fresh water to the Red Sea result in the excess evaporation as high as 205 cm (81 in) per year and high salinity with minimal seasonal variation.

Lake Baikal

Lake Baikal is in Southern Siberia in Russia, located between Irkutsk Oblast to the northwest and the Buryat Republic to the southeast, near the city of Irkutsk. It is also known as the "Blue Eye of Siberia". It contains more water than all the North American Great Lakes combined.

Lake Baikal

At 1,637 metres (5,371 ft), Lake Baikal is the deepest lake in the world, and the largest freshwater lake in the world by volume, holding approximately twenty percent of the world's total surface fresh water. Like Lake Tanganyika, Lake Baikal was formed in an ancient rift valley and therefore is long and crescent-shaped with a surface area (31,500 km^2) less than half that of Lake Superior or Lake Victoria. Baikal is home to more than 1,700 species of plants and animals, two thirds of which can be found nowhere else in the world and was declared a UNESCO World Heritage Site in 1996.

At more than 25 million years old, it is the oldest lake in the world. While Lake Baikal was known as the "North Sea" in historical Chinese texts, it was situated in the then Xionu territory and very little was known about Lake Baikal until the Trans-Siberian railway was built between 1896 and 1902. The scenic loop encircling Lake Baikal needed 200 bridges and 33 tunnels. As this railway was being built, a large hydrogeographical expedition headed by F.K. Drizhenko produced the first detailed atlas of the contours of Baikal's depths. The atlas demonstrated that Lake Baikal has more water than all of North America's Great Lakes combined —23,600 cubic kilometres (5,662.4 cu mi), about one fifth of the total fresh water on the earth.

At 636 kilometres (395 mi) long and 79 kilometres (49 mi) wide, Lake Baikal has the largest surface area of any freshwater lake in Asia (31,494 km^2) and is the deepest lake in the world (1,637 metres, previously measured at 1,620 metres). The bottom of the lake is 1,285 metres below sea level, but below this lies some 7 kilometres (4.3 mi) of sediment, placing the rift floor some 8-9 kilometres (more than 5 miles) below the surface: the deepest continental rift on Earth. In geological terms, the rift is young and active—it widens about two centimetres per year. The fault zone is also seismically active: there are hot springs in the area and notable earthquakes every few years. It drains into the Angara tributary of the Yenisei.

The Great Barrier Reef

Great Barrier Reef looks almost like a wall of perpendicular rock rising out of the sea - only it is not rock; it is coral. The Great Barrier Reef lies underwater and has snared many ships, including **Captain Cook's** in 1770. Though being one of the world's longest natural wonders, it unfortunately is also the most fragile around. It is a sweeping 2,000 kms in length, spanning along the **northeast coast of Australia**. It covers an area of 344,000 square kms and is made up of the skeletons of marine polyps that lived and died there, so it is generally lime-based. Sometimes the Great Barrier Reef is as close as 50 kms to the coast.

The Great Barrier Reef

The Great Barrier Reef consists of more than 3000 reefs spanning from 1 hectare to 10,000 hectares in area and is mainly made up of coral. The reef, however, is not just about polyps - dead or alive - they are also large numbers of different forms of **marine life**. There are colourful and exotic fishes, countless shellfish and other fanciful creatures. It abounds in wildlife. The variety of marine life ranges from nearly microscopic fishes to that of the larger fishes like the whale and the sharks.

There are more than 1500 species of fish, 4000 types of mollusk and, because of the abundance of fish, the reef is also home to more than 200 species of birds. The Great Barrier Reef houses anything and everything that thrives in shallow warm water.

It is also the only collection of organisms visible from Earth's orbit. It was declared a **World Heritage** in 1981. However, conditions like pollution, climatic change and various forms of human intrusion severely threaten its survival and continuance.

The Deep Sea Vents

Deep-sea vents are also known as deepwater seeps, deep-sea springs, **hydro-thermal vents** and blacksmokers. Found at **ocean floor**, they are formed by volcanic and tectonic activity in areas where huge hostile plates are unite or spread apart. Magma erupts along the margins of these plates, usually slowly, but sometimes with such ferocity that it creates instant lava lakes.

The Deep Sea Vents

Black smokers were first discovered in 1977 around the Galápagos Islands by the National Oceanic and Atmospheric Administration by using a small submersible vehicle called Alvin which first took photographs of these vents. Today, black smokers are known to exist in the Atlantic and Pacific Oceans, at an average depth of 2100 metres.

Because no sunlight reaches the depths where the vents are found, these underwater wonders are visible only in the floodlights of a manned submersible. Pitch darkness, poison gas, heavy metals, extreme acidity, enormous pressure, frigid and searing water prevails at the deep seafloor which literally reminds us of hell.

Yet amazing communities of life exist at these vents and the inhabitants are perhaps the most fascinating of all the world's underwater wonders from a scientific perspective. Blind shrimp, giant white crabs, and a variety of tubeworms are just some of the more than 300 species of **vent organisms** that have been identified by biologists so far. The most striking fact is about the food chain that functions without sunlight. As it was believed earlier that only sunlight, through photosynthesis, could support life on Earth. But, at the vents, however, life begins with bacteria that metabolize hydrogen sulfide. The bacteria, in turn, become food for the other animals in the vent society.

One of the peculiar residents of these vents are the giant red-tipped tube worms-12-foot-tall creatures whose 300,000 tentacles strain food from the water. Equally fascinating residents include pink ventfish, **sea cucumbers**, sponges, and brittle stars, flowerlike animals that use their fine appendages to anchor themselves to rocks.

Seven Forgotten Natural Wonders of the World

The **creations of nature** have always remained a mystery to the mankind. It is really beyond the perception and comprehension of human mind how Supreme Nature has continued with its miraculous creations! Nature sometimes seems to be an invisible artist or painter who paints magnificent landscapes with one stroke of his brush; these landscapes are either vibrant with colours or are brown, grey and dark with rugged and ravaged features. Sometimes Nature seems to be at its peculiar fancy -playing the role of a creator or destroyer- inventing and devastating at his omnipotent will.

The list of **seven forgotten natural wonders** includes those majestic creations of nature which have inspired awe and admiration of human minds in the recent past.

Angel Falls

Angel Falls is the world's highest free-falling waterfall at 979 m (3,212 ft), with a clear drop of 807 m (2,647 ft). It is located in the Canaima National Park, in the Gran Sabana region of Bolivar State, Venezuela. The height of the falls is so great that before getting anywhere near the ground, the water is buffeted by the strong winds and turned into mist.

Angel Falls

The base of the falls feeds into the Kerep river (alternately known as the Rio Gauya) which flows into the Churun River, a tributary of the Carrao River. In the indigenous Pemon language Angel Falls is called Kerepakupai meru meaning "waterfall of the deepest place".

Sir Walter Raleigh is sometimes said to have discovered Angel Falls, but these claims are considered "far-fetched". They were sighted in 1912 by the Venezuelan explorer Ernesto Sanchez La Cruz, but he did not publicize his discovery. They were not known to the outside world until the American aviator James "Jimmie" Crawford Angel flew over them on 16 November 1933 on a flight while he was searching for a valuable ore bed.

Returning on 9 October 1937, Angel tried to land his Flamingo monoplane "El Rio Caroni" atop Auyan-tepui but the plane was damaged when the wheels sunk into the marshy ground and he and his three companions, including his wife Marie, were forced to descend the tepui on foot. It took them 11 days to make their way back to civilization but news of their adventure spread and the waterfall was named 'Angel Falls" in his honour.

Angel's plane remained on top of the tepuy for 33 years before being lifted out by helicopter. The first recorded human to reach the river that feeds the falls was the Latvian explorer Aleksandrs Laime, also known as Alejandro Laime to the native Pemon tribe. He made the ascent of Auyan-tepui in 1955. He also reached Angel's plane on the same trip, 18 years after the crash landing. He gave the name of the river after one of the most beautiful rivers in Latvia, the river Gauja. While the indigenous name of the falls is rarely used anymore, the Pemon given name of the river, Kerep, is still widely used.

The Bay of Fundy

Bay of Fundy, large tidal inlet of the North Atlantic Ocean, separating the provinces of New Brunswick and Nova Scotia, and bordering on SE Maine. It is about 275 km (about 171 mi) long and up to 80 km (about 50 mi) wide. In the E, Fundy divides into two arms, Chignecto Bay on the N and Minas Channel (which leads into Minas Basin) on the S. The funnel effect of these narrowing arms increases the tidal range of the bay, and at times the water in the arms rises by as much as 18 m (about 60 ft), creating one of the world's highest tides. The tidal surge in Chignecto Bay produces a large crested wave, or bore, ranging to 1.8 m (about 6 ft) in height, in the lower Petitcodiac R. The rising tide in Fundy proper creates a "reversing falls" on the lower Saint John R., at Saint John, N.B. Passamaquoddy Bay, a W arm of Fundy, forms part of the boundary between New Brunswick and Maine. Although Fundy is very deep, navigation is difficult because of the rapid rise and fall of the tide. Major deepwater harbours are located at St. John and at Digby and Hantsport, N.S. Fundy National Park borders the bay in New Brunswick. The bay was discovered by the French explorer Pierre du Guast, sieur de Monts, in 1604.

The Bay of Fundy

Iguazu Falls

Iguazu Falls, Iguassu Falls, or Iguacu Falls are waterfalls of the Iguazu River located on the border of the Brazilian state of Parana and the Argentine province of Misiones. The falls divide the river into the upper and lower Iguazu.

Iguazu Falls

Legend has it that a god planned to marry a beautiful aborigine named Nalpi, who fled with her mortal lover Taroba in a canoe. In rage, the god sliced the river creating the waterfalls, condemning the lovers to an eternal fall. The first European to find the falls was the Spanish Conquistador Alvar Nunez Cabeza de Vaca in 1541, after whom one of the falls in the Argentine side is named.

The falls were rediscovered by Boselli at the end of the nineteenth century, and one of the Argentinian falls is named after him. The waterfall system consists of 275 falls along 2.7 kilometres (1.67 miles) of the Iguazu River.

Some of the individual falls are up to 82 metres (269 ft) in height, though the majority are about 64 metres (210 ft).

The Garganta del Diablo (Devil's Throat in English), a U-shaped 150-metre-wide and 700-metre-long (490 by 2300 feet) cliff, is the most impressive of all, and marks the border between Argentina and Brazil. Two thirds of the falls are within Argentine territory. About 900 metres of the 2.7-kilometre length does not have water flowing over it. The edge of the basalt cap recedes only 3 mm per year.

The water falling over Iguazu in peak flow has a surface area of about 40 ha (1.3 million ft^2) whilst Victoria in peak flow has a surface area of over 55 ha (1.8 million ft^2). By comparison, Niagara has a surface area of under 18.3 ha (600,000 ft^2). Victoria's annual peak flow is also greater than Iguazu's annual peak-9100 m^3/s versus 6500—though in times of extreme flood the two have recorded very similar maximum water discharge (well in excess of 12000 m^3/s). Niagara's annual peak flow is about 2800 m^3/s, although an all-time peak of 6800 has been recorded. Iguazu and Victoria fluctuate more greatly in their flow rate. Mist rises between 30 and 150 m (100 and 500 ft) from Iguazu's Garganta do Diabo, and over 300 in (1,000 ft) above Victoria (sometimes over 600 m).

Krakatoa Island

Krakatoa (Indonesian name: Krakatau, Portuguese name: Krakatao) is a volcanic island in the Sunda Strait between Java and Sumatra in **Indonesia.** It has erupted repetitively massively and with devastating consequences throughout recorded history. The best known eruption occurred in a chain of huge explosions on August 26-27, 1883. Several years of regional seismicity resulted in the famous caldera-forming eruption of August 1883.

Krakatoa Island

The 1883 eruption threw away more than 25 cubic kilometres of rock, ash, and pumice and generated the loudest sound ever historically reported - the cataclysmic explosion was distinctly heard as far away as Perth in Australia. Near Krakatoa, according to estimated records, 165 villages and towns were ruined and 132 seriously damaged, at least 36,417 people died, and many thousands were injured by the eruption, mostly in the tsunamis which followed the explosion. The eruption produced erratic weather and spectacular sunsets throughout the world for many months afterwards, as a result of sunlight reflected from suspended dust particles ejected by the volcano high into Earth's atmosphere. It has been described as one of the deadliest eruptions of the world.

Recent eruptions of **Krakatoa** have been at Anak Krakatau, an island that emerged in 1927. One tourist was killed and five more injured by an explosion at Anak Krakatau in 1993. Anak Krakatau is undergoing relatively dormant periods, lasting at least a couple days, punctuated by periods of nearly continuous eruption. After having 44 years rest, the child of Krakatoa appeared in December 1927 and it is expanding until now. Now the child of Krakatoa has reached approximately 200 m above sea level with the diametre of 2 kilometres.

The way to reach there is from Canti located in Kalianda. After about an hour's driving from Bandar Lampung, the boats take the tourists to the Krakatoa area.

Ancient Krakatoa was estimated 2,000 metres in height and radius of 9 kms.

Its great eruption happened in pre history in 416 as documented in the ancient Javanese book "Pustaka Raja", and left 3 islands safe i.e. Rakata, Sertung and Panjang Islands.

Mount Fuji of Japan

Fuji or Fujiyama, also Fuji-no-Yama or Fujisan, is in Japan, S Honshu Island, near Tokyo. Fuji, the celebrated sacred volcano and the highest mountain in Japan, rises as a cone to a height of 3776 m (12,389 ft) above sea level, with the apex broken by a cone-shaped crater 610 m (2000 ft) in diametre. The S slopes extend to the shore of Suruga Bay, and the isolated peak can be seen from many of the outlying prefectures. The mountain is part of Fuji-Hakone-Izu National Park. According to legend, Fuji arose from the plain during a single night in 286 BC. The most recent recorded eruption of Fuji lasted from Nov. 24, 1707, until Jan. 22, 1708. As the sacred mountain of Japan, it is visited annually by thousands of pilgrims from all parts of the country, and numerous shrines and temples are on its slopes. Fuji is also revered in Japanese literature and art.

Mount Fuji of Japan

Mount Kilimanjaro

Kilimanjaro, the highest mountain in Africa, located in northeastern Tanzania, near the border with Kenya. Kilimanjaro is a dormant volcano. Its two peaks stand 11 km (7 mi) apart and are connected by a broad ridge. Kibo, the higher peak, rises to 5,895 m (19,341 ft) above sea level, and the summit of Mawensi is 5,149 m (16,893 ft) above sea level. Although Kilimanjaro lies 3° south of the equator, an ice cap covers the crater of Kibo year-round; this ice cap is pierced by several small craters. "The Snows of Kilimanjaro" (1938), one of the most famous stories of American writer Ernest Hemingway, is set in the region. Kilimanjaro has a number of different vegetation zones on its steep slopes. Coffee and plantains are grown on the lower slopes of Kilimanjaro. The mountain was successfully scaled for the first time in 1889 by German geographer Hans Meyer and Austrian mountain climber Ludwig Purtscheller.

Mount Kilimanjaro

Niagara Falls

Niagara Falls are massive waterfalls on the Niagara River, straddling the international border separating the Canadian province of Ontario and the U.S. state of New York. The falls are 17 miles (27 km) north-northwest of Buffalo, New York, 75 miles (120 km) south-southeast of Toronto, Ontario, between the twin cities of Niagara Falls, Ontario, and Niagara Falls, New York.

Niagara Falls

Niagara Falls is composed of two major sections separated by Goat Island: Horseshoe Falls, on the Canadian side of the border and American Falls on the United States side. The smaller Bridal Veil Falls also is located on the American side, separated from the main falls by Luna Island. Niagara Falls were formed when glaciers receded at the end of the Wisconsin glaciation (the last ice age), and water from the newly-formed Great Lakes carved a path through the Niagara Escarpment en route to the Atlantic Ocean. While not exceptionally high, the Niagara Falls are very wide. More than six million cubic feet (168,000 m^3) of water fall over the crest line every minute in high flow, and almost 4 million cubic feet (110,000 m³) on average. It is the most powerful waterfall in North America.

Niagara Falls is divided into the Horseshoe Falls and the American Falls. The Horseshoe Falls drop about 173 feet (53 m), the height of the American Falls varies between 70-100 feet (21 m) because of the presence of giant boulders at its base. The larger Horseshoe Falls are about 2,600 feet (792 m) wide, while the American Falls are 1,060 feet (323 m) wide. The volume of water approaching the falls during peak flow season is 202,000 cubic feet per second (5,720 m³/s).

By comparison Africa's spectacular Victoria Falls has over 15 million cubic feet (424,750 m³) of water falling over its crest line each minute during the peak of the wet season (250,000 cu ft/7,079 m³ per second). Since the flow is a direct function of the Lake Erie water elevation, it typically peaks in late spring or early summer. During the summer months, 100,000 cubic feet per second (2,832 m³/s) of water actually traverses the Falls. The most complete views of Niagara Falls are available from the Canadian shoreline.

Seven Forgotten Modern Wonders of the World

The Seven forgotten modern wonders of the world account for the brilliance of the human mind, its perceptive power and adroit endeavors, which were considered as some of the **greatest wonders of the world**, but not great enough to leave behind an indelible impression on humanity's mind, and lost to the other greater and stupendous works of the human imagination. The **momentous works** of art and architecture by the humans and their ability to capture in realistic frame baffled travellers and onlookers from times immemorial and with the advance of the science and technology, engineering skills and **construction facilities**, the human hands began to carve out of their minds, edifices which made the world pleasanter and beautiful. The Seven forgotten modern wonders of the world are part of such grand endeavors, and although somewhere lost from the minds of humans, are unique and intriguing in their own special ways.

The Clock Tower (Big Ben)

Big Ben tower clock famous for its accuracy and for its massive bell (weighing more than 13 tons). It is housed in St. Stephen's Tower, at the northern end of the Houses of Parliament, in the London borough of Westminster. In coordination with the Royal Greenwich Observatory, the chimes of Big Ben have been broadcast as a feature of the BBC's daily time signal since 1924, with brief interruptions (owing to repairwork) in 1934 and 1956. The clock was designed by Edmund Beckett Denison and built by E.J. Dent and, later, Frederick Dent. The name of the clock is said by some historians to stand for Sir Benjamin Hall, the commissioner of

The Clock Tower (Big Ben)

works. At the time of the clock and bell's installation in 1859, the name applied only to the bell, but it eventually came to indicate the clock itself. In 1956 the clock mechanism was restored and repaired. The hands of the clock are 9 and 14 feet (2.7 and 4.3 metres) long, respectively, and the clock tower rises to 320 feet (98 metres). The bell was cast by George Mears of Whitechapel and pulled to the tower by a wagon team of 16 horses. Shortly after it was installed, it developed a crack and was kept out of service until its repair in 1862.St. Stephen's Tower once contained a prison cell where "rioters" were confined. The leader of the woman suffrage movement, Emmeline Pankhurst, was placed in the cell in 1902 after demonstrating nearby.

The Eiffel Tower

The Eiffel Tower is an iron tower built on the Champ de Mars beside the Seine River in Paris. The tower has become a global icon of France and is one of the most recognizable structures in the world.

The Eiffel Tower

Named after its designer, engineer Gustave Eiffel, the Eiffel Tower is the tallest building in Paris and one of the most recognized structures in the world. More than 200,000,000 have visited the tower since its construction in 1889, including 6,719,200 in 2006, making it the most visited paid monument in the world. Including the 24 m (79 ft) antenna, the structure is 325 m (1,063 ft) high (since 2000), which is equivalent to about 81 levels in a conventional building.

The metal structure of the Eiffel Tower weighs 7,300 tonnes while the entire structure including non-metal components is approximately 10,000 tonnes. Depending on the ambient temperature, the top of the tower may shift away from the sun by up to 18 cm (7 in) because of thermal expansion of the metal on the side facing the sun. The tower also sways 6-7 cm (2-3 in) in the wind. The tower has a mass less than the mass of the air contained in a cylinder of the same dimensions that is 324 metres high and 88.3 metres in radius. The weight of the tower is 10,100 tonnes compared to 10,265 tonnes of air.

The first and second levels are accessible by stairways and lifts. At the first platform the stairs continue up from the east tower and the third level summit is only accessible by lift. From the first or second platform the stairs are open for anyone to ascend or descend regardless of whether they have purchased a lift ticket or stair ticket. The actual count of stairs includes 9 steps to the ticket booth at the base, 328 steps to the first level, 340 steps to the second level and 18 steps to the lift platform on the second level. When exiting the lift at the third level there are 15 more steps to ascend to the upper observation platform. The step count is printed periodically on the side of the stairs to give an indication of progress of ascent. The majority of the ascent allows for an unhindered view of the area directly beneath and around the tower although some short stretches of the stairway are enclosed.

The Gateway Arch

The Gateway Arch, also known as the Gateway to the West, is an integral part of the Jefferson National Expansion Memorial and the iconic image of St. Louis, Missouri. It was designed by Finnish-American architect Eero Saarinen and structural engineer Hannskarl Bandel. It stands 630 feet (192 m) tall, and is 630 feet (192 m) wide at its base, making it the tallest monument in the United States.

The Gateway Arch

The cross-sections of its legs are equilateral triangles, narrowing from 54 feet (16.5 m) per side at the base to 17 feet (5.2 m) at the top. Each wall consists of a stainless steel skin covering reinforced concrete from ground level to 300 feet (91 m), with carbon steel and bar from 300 feet (91 m) to the peak. The interior of the Arch is hollow and contains a unique transport system leading to an observation deck at the top. The interior of the Arch also contains two emergency stairwells of 1076 steps each, in the event of a need to evacuate the Arch or if a problem develops with the tram system.

The base of each leg at ground level had an engineering tolerance of one sixty-fourth of an inch or the two legs would not meet at the top. During construction, both legs were built up simultaneously. When the time came to connect both legs together at the apex, thermal expansion of the sunward facing south leg, prevented it from aligning precisely with the north leg. This alignment problem was solved when the Saint Louis City Fire Department sprayed the south leg with water from firehoses until it had cooled to the point where it aligned with the north leg. It is the tallest habitable structure in St. Louis (taller than One Metropolitan Square, the tallest building), and the second tallest in Missouri (behind One Kansas City Place in Kansas City).

Near the top of the arch, the rider exits the compartment and climbs a slight grade to enter the arched observation area. Small windows, almost invisible from the ground, allow views across the Mississippi River and southern Illinois with its prominent Mississippian culture mounds to the east at Cahokia, and the City of Saint Louis and St. Louis County to the west beyond the city. On a clear day, one can see up to thirty miles (48 km).

The Aswan High Dam

Arabic As-Sadd al-'Ali, rock-fill dam across the Nile River, at Aswan, Egypt, completed in 1970 (and formally inaugurated in January 1971) at a cost of about $1 billion. The dam, 364 feet (111 m) high, with a crest length of 12,562 feet (3,830 m) and a volume of 57,940,000 cubic yards (44,300,000 cubic m), impounds a reservoir, Lake Nasser, that has a gross capacity of 5.97 trillion cubic feet (169 billion cubic m). Of the Nile's total annual discharge, some 2.6 trillion cubic feet (74 billion cubic m) of water have been allocated by treaty between Egypt and The Sudan, with about 1.96 trillion cubic feet (55.5 billion cubic m) apportioned to Egypt and the remainder to The Sudan. Lake Nasser backs up

The Aswan High Dam

the Nile about 200 miles (320 km) in Egypt and almost 100 miles (160 km) farther upstream (south) in The Sudan; creation of the reservoir necessitated the costly relocation of the ancient Egyptian temple complex of Abu Simbel, which would otherwise have been submerged. Ninety thousand Egyptian fellahin (peasants) and Sudanese Nubian nomads had to be relocated. Fifty thousand Egyptians were transported to the Kawm Umbu valley, 30 miles (50 km) north of Aswan, to form a new agricultural zone called Nubaria; most of the Sudanese were resettled around Khashm al-Qirbah, Sudan. The Aswan High Dam yields enormous benefits to the economy of Egypt. For the first time in history, the annual Nile flood can be controlled by man. The dam impounds the floodwaters, releasing them when needed to maximize their utility on irrigated land, to water hundreds of thousands of new acres, to improve navigation both above and below Aswan, and to generate enormous amounts of electric power (the dam's 12 turbines can generate 10 billion kilowatt-hours annually). The reservoir, which has a depth of 300 feet (90 m) and averages 14 miles (22 km) in width, supports a fishing industry.The Aswan High Dam has produced several negative side effects, however, chief of which is a gradual decrease in the fertility and hence the productivity of Egypt's riverside agricultural lands. This is because of the dam's complete control of the Nile's annual flooding. Much of the flood and its load of rich fertilizing silt is now impounded in reservoirs and canals; the silt is thus no longer deposited by the Nile's rising waters on farmlands. Egypt's annual application of about 1 million tons of artificial fertilizers is an inadequate substitute for the 40 million tons of silt formerly deposited annually by the Nile flood.Completed in 1902, with its crest raised in 1912 and 1933, an earlier dam 4 miles (6 km) downstream from the Aswan High Dam holds back about 174.2 billion cubic feet (4.9 billion cubic m) of water from the tail of the Nile flood in the late autumn. Once one of the largest dams in the world, it is 7,027 feet (2,142 m) long and is pierced by 180 sluices that formerly passed the whole Nile flood, with its heavy load of silt.

The Hoover Dam

Hoover Dam, also known as Boulder Dam, is a concrete arch-gravity dam in the Black Canyon of the Colorado River, on the border between the U.S. states of Arizona and Nevada. When completed in 1935, it was both the world's largest electric power producing facility and the world's largest concrete structure.

The Hoover Dam

The dam, located 30 miles (48 km) southeast of Las Vegas, is named after Herbert Hoover, who played an instrumental role in its construction, first as Secretary of Commerce and then later as President of the United States. Construction began in 1931 and was completed in 1935, more than two years ahead of schedule.

To protect the construction site from flooding, two cofferdams were constructed. Construction of the upper cofferdam began in September 1932, even though the river had not yet been diverted.

A temporary horseshoe-shaped dike protected the cofferdam on the Nevada side of the river. After the Arizona tunnels were completed, and the river diverted, the work was completed much faster. Once the coffer dams were in place and the construction site dewatered, excavation for the dam foundation began. For the dam to rest on solid rock, it was necessary to remove all loose material until solid rock was reached. Work on the foundation excavations was completed in June 1933. During excavations for the foundations, approximately 1,500,000 yd^3 (1,150,000 m$^{3)}$ of material was removed, including material removed in canyon wall stripping operations.

To divert the river's flow around the construction site, four diversion tunnels were driven through the canyon walls, two on the Nevada side and two on the Arizona side. These tunnels were 56 feet (17.07 m) in diametre. Their combined length was nearly 16,000 feet (4877 m, more than three miles). Tunneling began at the lower portals of the Nevada tunnels in May 1931. Shortly after, work began on two similar tunnels in the Arizona canyon wall. In March 1932, work began on lining the tunnels with concrete. First the base or invert was poured. Gantry cranes, running on rails through the entire length of each tunnel were used to place the concrete. The sidewalls were poured next. Movable sections of steel forms were used for the sidewalls. Finally, using pneumatic guns, the overheads were filled in. The concrete lining is 3 feet (914.4 mm) thick, reducing the finished tunnel diametre to 50 ft (15.24 in).

Mount Rushmore National Memorial

Mount Rushmore National Memorial, near Keystone, South Dakota, is a monumental granite sculpture by Gutzon Borglum, located within the United States Presidential Memorial that represents the first 150 years of the history of the United States of America with 60-foot (18 m) sculptures of the heads of former United States presidents (left to right): George Washington (1732-1799), Thomas Jefferson (1743-1826), Theodore Roosevelt (1858-1919), and Abraham Lincoln (1809-1865). The entire memorial covers 1,278.45 acres (5.17 km²) and is 5,725 feet (1,745 m) above sea level.

Mount Rushmore National Memorial

Between October 4, 1927, and October 31, 1941, Gutzon Borglum and 400 workers sculpted the colossal 60-foot (18 m) carvings of U.S. presidents George Washington, Thomas Jefferson,

Theodore Roosevelt, and Abraham Lincoln to represent the first 150 years of American history. These presidents were selected by Borglum because of their role in preserving the Republic and expanding its territory. The image of Thomas Jefferson was originally intended to appear in the area at Washington's right, but after the work there was begun, the rock was found unsuitable, so the work to that point on the Jefferson figure was dynamited, and a new figure was sculpted to Washington's left.

Ten years of redevelopment work culminated with the completion of extensive visitor facilities and sidewalks in 1998, such as a Visitor Centre, Museum, and the Presidential Trail. Maintenance of the memorial annually requires mountain climbers to monitor and seal cracks.

Mount Rushmore is largely composed of granite. The memorial is carved on the northwest margin of the Harney Peak granite batholith in the Black Hills of South Dakota, so the geologic formations of the heart of the Black Hills region are also evident at Mount Rushmore.

Borglum selected Mount Rushmore as the site for several reasons. The rock of the mountain is composed of smooth, fine-grained granite. The durable granite erodes only 1 inch (25 mm) every 10,000 years, indicating that it was sturdy enough to support sculpting. In addition, it was the tallest mountain in the region, looming to a height of 5,725 feet (1,745 m) above sea level. Because the mountain faces the southeast, the workers also had the advantage of sunlight for most of the day.

7

The Petronas Towers

The Petronas Twin Towers (also known as the Petronas Towers or Twin Towers), in Kuala Lumpur, Malaysia were the world's tallest buildings, before being surpassed by the Taipei 101. However, the towers are still the tallest twin buildings in the world.

The Petronas Towers

Designed by Argentine-American architect Cesar Pelli, the Petronas Towers were completed in 1998 and became the tallest buildings in the world on the date of completion. The 88-floor towers are constructed largely of reinforced concrete, with a steel and glass facade designed to resemble motifs found in Islamic art, a reflection of Malaysia's Muslim religion. They were built on the site of Kuala Lumpur's race track. Because of the depth of the bedrock, the buildings were built on the world's deepest foundations. The 120-metre foundations were built by Bachy Soletanche, and required massive amounts of concrete. In an unusual move, a different construction company was hired for each of the towers.

Due to a lack of steel and the huge cost of importing steel, the towers were constructed on a cheaper radical design of super high-strength reinforced concrete. High-strength concrete is a material familiar to Asian contractors and twice as effective as steel in sway reduction; however, it makes the building twice as heavy on its foundation than a comparable steel building. Supported by 23-by-23 metre concrete cores and an outer ring of widely-spaced super columns, the towers use a sophisticated structural system that accommodates its slender profile and provides from 1300 to 2000 square metres of column-free office space per floor. Spanning 17 acres below the building has the KLCC park with jogging and walking paths, a fountain with incorporated light show, wading pools, and a children's playground.

The towers feature a skybridge (constructed by Kukdong Engineering & Construction) between the two towers on 41st and 42nd floors, which is the highest 2-storey bridge in the world. The bridge is 170 m above the ground and 58 m long, weighing 750 tons. The same floor is also known as the podium, since visitors desiring to go to higher levels have to change elevators here. The skybridge also acts as a safety device, so that in the event of a fire or other emergency in one tower, tenants can evacuate by crossing the skybridge to the other tower.

Seven Forgotten Wonders of the Medieval Mind

Out of sight is out of mind – perhaps this has been the fate of the **Seven forgotten medieval wonders of the world**, which in the past had indeed inspired awe, admiration and respect in the heart of onlookers down the centuries after its creation but lost their importance to test of time. While some of these Seven forgotten medieval wonders of the world got eroded and destroyed to be converted to the state of ruins, some others lost in the competition with the more excellent works of human creativity and engineering feats that followed.

Medieval era around the world sparked the flame of intelligence and zeal for creativity, evident in the wondrous works of the time. But the turn of events and science since the time of the medieval to the modern world has been dramatic, leading to more extraordinary works, dwarfing the **marvels of the medieval world**.

Abu Simbel Temple

Abu Simbel is an archaeological site comprising two massive rock temples in southern Egypt on the western bank of Lake Nasser about 290 km southwest of Aswan. It is part of the UNESCO World Heritage Site known as the "Nubian Monuments", which run from Abu Simbel downriver to Philae.

Abu Simbel Temple

The twin temples were originally carved out of the mountainside during the reign of Pharaoh Ramesses II in the 13th century BC, as a lasting monument to himself and his queen Nefertari, to commemorate his alleged victory at the Battle of Kadesh, and to intimidate his Nubian neighbours. However, the complex was relocated in its entirety in the 1960s, on on an artificial hill made from a domed structure, high above the Aswan dam reservoir.

Construction of the temple complex started in approximately

1244 BC and lasted for about 20 years, until 1224 BC. Known as the "Temple of Ramses, beloved by Amun", it was one of six rock temples erected in Nubia during the long reign of Ramses II.

The Great Temple at Abu Simbel, which took about twenty wars to build, was completed around year 24 of the reign of Ramesses the Great. It was dedicated to the gods Amun Ra, Ra-Horakhty, and Ptah, as well as to the deified Ramesses himself. It is generally considered the grandest and most beautiful of the temples commissioned during the reign of Ramesses II, and one of the most beautiful in Egypt.

Four colossal 20 metre statues of the pharaoh with the double crown of Upper and Lower Egypt decorate the facade of the temple which is 35 metres wide and is topped by a frieze with 22 baboons, worshippers of the sun and flank the entrance. The colossal statues were sculptured directly from the rock in which the temple was located before it was moved.

The inner part of the temple has the same triangular layout that most ancient Egyptian temples follow, with rooms decreasing in size from the entrance to the sanctuary. The temple is complex in structure and quite unusual because of its many side chambers. The hypostyle hall (sometimes also called pronaos) is 18 metres long and 16.7 metres wide and is supported by eight huge Osirid pillars depicting the deified Ramesses linked to the god Osiris, the god of the Underworld, to indicate the everlasting nature of the pharaoh.

Angkor Wat

Angkor Wat (or Angkor Vat), is a temple at Angkor, Cambodia, built for King Suryavarman II in the early 12th century as his state temple and capital city. As the best-preserved temple at the site, it is the only one to have remained a significant religious centre since its foundation - first Hindu, dedicated to Vishnu, then Buddhist. The temple is the epitome of the high classical style of Khmer architecture. It has become a symbol of Cambodia, appearing on its national flag, and it is the country's prime attraction for visitors.

Angkor Wat

The outer wall, 1024 by 802 m and 4.5 m high, is surrounded by a 30 m apron of open ground and a moat 190 m wide. Access to the temple is by an earth bank to the east and a sandstone causeway to the west; the latter, the main entrance, is a later addition, possibly replacing a wooden bridge.

The outer wall encloses a space of 820,000 square metres (203 acres), which besides the temple proper was originally occupied by the city and, to the north of the temple, the royal palace. Like all secular buildings of Angkor, these were built of perishable materials rather than of stone, so nothing remains of them except the outlines of some of the streets. A 350 m causeway connects the western gopura to the temple proper, with naga balustrades and six sets of steps leading down to the city on either side.

The temple stands on a terrace raised higher than the city. It is made of three rectangular galleries rising to a central tower, each level higher than the last. Mannikka interprets these galleries as being dedicated to the king, Brahma, the moon, and Vishnu. Each gallery has a gopura at each of the points, and the two inner galleries each have towers at their corners, forming a quincunx with the central tower. Because the temple faces west, the features are all set back towards the east, leaving more space to be filled in each enclosure and gallery on the west side; for the same reason the west-facing steps are shallower than those on the other sides.

The outer gallery measures 187 by 215 m, with pavilions rather than towers at the corners. The gallery is open to the outside of the temple, with columned half-galleries extending and buttressing the structure.

3

Taj Mahal of Agra

The Taj Mahal, is a mausoleum located in Agra, India, that was built under Mughal Emperor Shah Jahan in memory of his favourite wife, Mumtaz Mahal. While the white domed marble and tile mausoleum is most familiar, Taj Mahal is an integrated symmetric complex of structures that was completed around 1648. Ustad Ahmad Lahauri is generally considered to be the principal designer of the Taj Mahal.

Taj Mahal of Agra

The focus of the Taj Mahal is the white marble tomb, which stands on a square plinth consisting of a symmetrical building with an iwan, an arch-shaped doorway, topped by a large dome. Like most Mughal tombs, basic elements are Persian in origin.

The base of the Taj is a large, multi-chambered structure.

The base structure is a large, multi-chambered structure. The base is essentially a cube with chamfered edges and is roughly 55 metres on each side. On the long sides, a massive pishtaq, or vaulted archway, frames the diwan with a similar arch-shaped balcony.

The interior chamber of the Taj Mahal steps far beyond traditional decorative elements. Here the inlay work is not pietra dura, but lapidary of precious and semiprecious gemstones. The inner chamber is an octagon with the design allowing for entry from each face, though only the south garden-facing door is used. The interior walls are about 25 metres high and topped by a "false" interior dome decorated with a sun motif. Eight pishtaq arches define the space at ground level. As with the exterior, each lower pishtaq is crowned by a second pishtaq about midway up the wall.

The four central upper arches form balconies or viewing areas and each balcony's exterior window has an intricate screen or jali cut from marble. In addition to the light from the balcony screens, light enters through roof openings covered by chattris at the corners. Each chamber wall has been highly decorated with dado bas relief, intricate lapidary inlay and refined calligraphy panels, reflecting in miniature detail the design elements seen throughout the exterior of the complex. The octagonal marble screen or jali which borders the cenotaphs is made from eight marble panels. Each panel has been carved through with intricate pierce work. The remaining surfaces have been inlaid with semiprecious stones in extremely delicate detail, forming twining vines, fruits and flowers.

Mont Saint-Michel

Mont Saint-Michel is a rocky tidal island in Normandy, France. It is located approximately one kilometre off the country's north coast, at the mouth of the Couesnon River near Avranches.

Mont Saint-Michel was used in the sixth and seventh centuries as an Armorican stronghold of Romano-Breton culture and power, until it was ransacked by the Franks, thus ending the trans-channel culture that had stood since the departure of the Romans in AD 460

Mont Saint-Michel

Mont Saint-Michel was previously connected to the mainland via a thin natural land bridge, which before modernization was covered at high tide and revealed at low tide. Thus, Mont Saint-Michel has been compromised by several developments.

Over the centuries, the coastal flats have been polderised to create pasture. Thus the distance between the shore and the south coast of Mont- Saint-Michel has decreased.

Before the construction of the first monastic establishment in the 8th century, the island was called Mont Tombe.

According to legend, the archangel Michael appeared to St. Aubert, bishop of Avranches, in 708 and instructed him to build a church on the rocky islet. Aubert repeatedly ignored the angel's instruction, until Michael burned a hole in the bishop's skull with his finger.

The mount gained strategic significance in 933 when William "Long Sword", Duke of Normandy, annexed the Cotentin Peninsula, definitively placing the mount in Normandy. It is depicted in the Bayeux Tapestry, which commemorates the 1066 Norman conquest of England. Ducal patronage financed the spectacular Norman architecture of the abbey in subsequent centuries.

In 1067, the monastery of Mont Saint-Michel gave its support to duke William of Normandy in his claim to the throne of England. It was rewarded with properties and grounds on the English side of the Channel, including a small island located at the west of Cornwall, which, modelled after the Mount, became a Norman priory named St Michael's Mount of Penzance.

During the Hundred Years' War the, English made repeated assaults on the island but were unable to seize it, partly due to the abbey's improved fortifications. Les Michelettes, two wrought-iron bombards left by the English in their failed 1423-24 siege of Mont Saint-Michel, are still displayed near the outer defense wall.

The Moai Statues

Moai are monolithic human figures carved from rock on the Polynesian island of Rapa Nui (Easter Island) between 1250 and 1500 CE. Nearly half are still at Rano Raraku, the main Moai quarry, but hundreds were transported from there and set on stone platforms called Ahu around the island's perimetre. Almost all Moai have overly large heads three-fifths the size of their bodies. The Moai are chiefly the 'living faces' (aringa ora) of deified ancestors. The statues still gazed inland across their clan lands when Europeans first visited the island, but most would be cast down during later conflicts between clans.

The Moai Statues

The statues' production and transportation is considered a remarkable intellectual, creative, and physical feat. The tallest Moai erected, called Paro, was almost 10 metres (33 ft) high and weighed 75 tonnes; the heaviest erected was a shorter but squatter Moai at Ahu Tonganki, weighing 86 tons; and one unfinished sculpture, if completed, would have been approximately 21 metres (69 ft) tall with a weight of about 270 tons.

The Moai are monolithic statues, their minimalist style related to forms found throughout Polynesia. Moai are carved in relatively flat planes, the faces bearing proud but enigmatic expressions. The over-large heads have heavy brows, elongated noses with a distinctive fish-hook shaped curl of the nostrils.

The lips protrude in a thin pout. Like the nose, the ears are elongated, and oblong in form. The jaw lines stand out against the truncated neck. The torsos are heavy, and sometimes the clavicles are subtly outlined in stone. The arms are carved in bas relief and rest against the body in various positions, hands and long slender fingers resting along the crests of the hips, meeting at the hami (loincloth), with the thumbs sometimes pointing towards the navel. Generally, the anatomical details of the backs are not detailed, but sometimes bear a ring and girdle motif on the buttocks and lower back. Except for one kneeling Moai, the statues do not have legs.

All but 53 of the 887 Moai known to date were carved from tuff (a compressed volcanic ash). At the end of carving they would rub the statue with pumice from Rano Raraku, where 394 Moai and incomplete Moai are still visible today (there are also 13 Moai carved from basalt, 22 from trachyte and 17 from fragile red scoria).

The Parthenon of Athens

The Acropolis of Athens is the best known acropolis (high city, The "Sacred Rock") in the world. Although there are many other acropoleis in Greece, the significance of the Acropolis of Athens is such that it is commonly known as The Acropolis without qualification. The Acropolis was formally proclaimed is the pre-eminent monument on the European Cultural Heritage list of monuments on 26 March 2007. The Acropolis is a flat-topped rock which rises 150 m (490 ft) above sea level in the city of Athens. It was also known as Cecropia, after the legendary serpent-man, Kekrops or Cecrops, the first Athenian king.

The Parthenon of Athens

Once into the Bronze Age, there is little doubt that a Mycenaean megaron must have stood on top of the hill, housing the local potentate and his household, guards, the local cult facilities and a number of workshops and ordinary habitations.

The compound was surrounded by a thick Cyclopean circuit wall, possibly between 4.5 m and 6 m in height, consisting of two parapets built with large stone blocks and cemented with an earth mortar called emplekton. The wall follows typical Mycenaean convention in that its gate was arranged obliquely, with a parapet and tower overhanging the incomers' right-hand side, thus facilitating defense. There were two lesser approaches up the hill on its north side, consisting of steep, narrow flights of steps cut in the rock.

Most of the major temples were rebuilt under the leadership of Pericles during the Golden Age of Athens (460-430 BC). Phidias, a great Athenian sculptor, and Ictinus and Callicrates, two famous architects, were responsible for the reconstruction. During the 5th century BC, the Acropolis gained its final shape.

The entrance to the Acropolis was a monumental gateway called the Propylaea. To the south of the entrance is the tiny Temple of Athena Nike. A bronze statue of Athena, sculpted by Phidias, originally stood at its centre. At the centre of the Acropolis is the Parthenon or Temple of Athena Parthenon (Athena the Virgin). East of the entrance and north of the Parthenon is the temple known as the Erechtheum. South of the platform that forms the top of the Acropolis there are also the remains of an outdoor theatre called Theatre of Dionysus. A few hundred metres away, there is the now partially reconstructed Theatre of Herodes Atticus.

7

The Shwedagon Pagoda

The Shwedagon Pagoda, also known as the Golden Pagoda, is a 98-metre (approx. 321.5 feet) gilded stupa located in Yangon, Burma. The pagoda lies to the west of Kandawgyi Lake, on Singuttara Hill, thus dominating the skyline of the city. It is the most sacred Buddhist pagoda for the Burmese with relics of the past four Buddhas enshrined within, namely the staff of

The Shwedagon Pagoda

Kakusandha, the water filter of Konagamana, a piece of the robe of Kassapa and eight hairs of Gautama, the historical Buddha.

Legend has it that the Shwedagon Pagoda is 2500 years old. Archaeologists believe the stupa was actually built sometime between the 6th and 10th centuries by the Mon, but this is a very controversial issue because according to the records by Buddhist monks it was built before Lord Buddha died in 486 BC.

There are four entrances (mouk) to the Paya that lead up a flight of steps to the platform (yin byin) on Siriguttara Hill. The eastern and southern approaches have vendors selling books, good luck charms, Buddha images, candles, gold leaf, incense sticks, prayer flags, streamers, miniature umbrellas and flowers. A pair of giant chinthe (leogryphs, mythical lions) guard the entrances and the image in the shrine at the top of the steps from the south is that of the second Buddha, Konagamana. The base or plinth of the stupa is made of bricks covered with gold plates. Above the base are terraces (pyissayan) that only monks and men can access. Next is the bell-shaped part (khaung laung bon) of the stupa. Above that is the turban (baung yit), then the inverted almsbowl (thabeik), inverted and upright lotus petals (kya hmauk kya hlan), the banana bud (nga pyaw bu) and then the crown. The crown or umbrella (hti) is tipped with 5,448 diamonds and 2,317 rubies. The very top, the diamond bud (sein bu) is tipped with a 76 carat (15 g) diamond.

The Gold seen on the stupa is made of genuine gold plates, covering the brick structure attached by traditional rivets. Myanmar people all over the country, as well as monarchs in its history, have donated gold to the pagoda to maintain it. It was started in the 15th century by the Mon Queen Shin Sawbu who gave her weight in gold and continues to this day.

www.ingramcontent.com/pod-product-compliance
Lightning Source LLC
LaVergne TN
LVHW051201080426
835508LV00021D/2744